Her Giving Journey

Women Who Inspire Generosity

Adriana Luna Carlos and **Hanna Olivas**
along with 4 inspiring authors

ISBN: 978-1-964619-60-6

TABLE OF CONTENTS

INTRODUCTION

Welcome to *Her Giving Journey: Women Who Inspire Generosity*, a heartfelt celebration of extraordinary women whose acts of kindness and generosity have sparked transformative change in their communities and beyond. In a world often focused on individual achievements, these remarkable stories remind us of the power of collective compassion and the ripple effects of selflessness.

In these pages, you'll meet women from diverse backgrounds, each with her unique abilities and resources, who have harnessed their strengths to uplift those around them. From local heroes to global changemakers, their journeys highlight the profound impact that generosity can have—not just on recipients, but on the givers themselves and the wider world.

As you delve into these inspiring narratives, you'll discover the creative ways these women have approached challenges, the obstacles they've overcome, and the enduring legacies they've created. Each story is a testament to the idea that generosity knows no boundaries and that small acts can lead to monumental changes.

Join us in exploring the remarkable journeys of these women. Let their stories inspire you to reflect on your own capacity for kindness and generosity, and consider how you, too, can make a difference. Together, we can cultivate a culture of giving that transcends borders and empowers us all to contribute to a brighter future.

Adriana Luna Carlos

Founder and CEO of SHE RISES STUDIOS & FENIX TV

https://www.linkedin.com/in/adriana-luna-carlos/
https://www.facebook.com/adrianalunacarlos
https://www.instagram.com/sherisesstudios_llc/
https://www.sherisesstudios.com/
https://fenixtv.app/

Adriana Luna Carlos is an accomplished web and graphic designer, author, and mentor with a passion for helping women succeed in life and business. With over 10 years of experience in graphic and web arts, Adriana has built a reputation as an innovative leader and entrepreneur. In 2020, she co-founded She Rises Studios, a multi-digital media company and publishing house that has helped countless clients achieve their branding and marketing goals. In 2023, she co-created FENIX TV, an online streaming platform that showcases stories of people breaking barriers, shattering stereotypes, and triumphing against the odds.

As an advocate for women's success, Adriana challenges her clients and mentees to strive for nothing less than excellence. She has a deep understanding of the insecurities and challenges that women often face in the business world and provides the guidance and resources needed to overcome them. Her success as a business leader and entrepreneur has made her a sought-after mentor and speaker at events around the world.

Through her work, Adriana has demonstrated a commitment to creating opportunities for women to succeed in business and life. Her passion for innovation, leadership, and women's empowerment has made her a respected figure in the business community, and her impact will undoubtedly continue to inspire and empower women for years to come.

A Generous Heart

By Adriana Luna Carlos

Generosity is often seen as an act of giving—whether it's time, resources, or a listening ear. But for me, generosity goes beyond these tangible offerings; it's about sharing the strength, lessons, and purpose life has instilled in us, especially during difficult times. My journey of giving has been less about material resources and more about sharing the resilience that comes from a life shaped by challenges, triumphs, and unwavering values.

I come from a family who truly values the worth of hard work. Growing up, our principle was simple yet powerful: "We say what we mean, and we do what we say." It's a saying that became my guiding light. It taught me the importance of commitment, the integrity behind every promise, and the satisfaction of seeing a job well done. This value rooted in action, rather than just words, shaped my journey and my approach to generosity.

As I grew older, I realized that my calling wasn't just about hard work; it was about creating spaces where others could thrive. I found purpose in inspiring and uplifting women, especially those who faced self-doubt or felt unseen. My career journey began with design and entrepreneurship, but it soon evolved into a larger mission—empowering women to believe in their own worth and to rise above limitations they once thought defined them.

A Generous Heart Requires a Strong Foundation

Generosity, for me, started with understanding my own worth and finding my voice. There was a time when I didn't always feel like I belonged, despite being surrounded by strong personalities. I thrived in school, loved helping others, but often forgot to extend that same compassion to myself. Through some of life's toughest lessons, I learned that true generosity must first include oneself. By investing in my own growth, I could then be of greater service to others.

One of the most profound ways I learned to give was by creating She Rises Studios. It wasn't just about providing services; it was about creating a safe space where women could find inspiration, tools, and community support to overcome their own challenges. Building this platform allowed me to channel my experiences into a form of generosity that continues to ripple outward. By supporting others in their personal and professional journeys, I realized that I was able to share more than just skills—I was sharing strength, empowerment, and a belief in their potential.

Giving Through Connection and Community

A generous life, I've found, is one that's grounded in authentic connections. It's about recognizing the power of a shared story, the comfort of knowing someone has walked a similar path, and the strength that comes from uplifting each other. The communities I've built, both professionally and personally, have reinforced my belief in the power of women supporting women.

Through She Rises Studios, I saw how creating a community driven by empowerment and shared experiences became a powerful way to give back. It was about more than services or products—it was about fostering an environment where women could lean on each other, share their wisdom, and grow together. The generosity of spirit that comes from these connections is profound; it fuels resilience, instills confidence, and brings a unique joy that only shared support can bring.

The Generosity of Sharing Our Stories

Perhaps the most meaningful act of generosity I've discovered is the courage to share my own story. It isn't always easy to revisit the difficult moments, the struggles, and the hard-earned lessons, but I've come to understand that there is immense power in doing so. When we share our journeys—the victories and the vulnerabilities—we give others permission to embrace their own paths fully. We remind them that they are not alone, and that within them lies the strength to rise above whatever challenges they face.

Through writing, speaking, and community events, I've seen firsthand how stories can inspire generosity in others. By giving our experiences a voice, we create ripples of empathy, hope, and encouragement. It's a form of giving that transcends material wealth—it's about passing on the gift of resilience, purpose, and belief in oneself.

Navigating the Challenges of Generosity

Generosity isn't always easy, and there have been moments in my journey when giving was met with its own set of challenges. One of the hardest lessons I've learned is that true generosity requires balance—it demands that we give from a place of abundance, not depletion. For years, I felt compelled to give everything I had, often prioritizing the needs of others over my own well-being. There's a unique joy that comes with giving, but when that giving comes at the expense of our own health or happiness, it can lead to burnout.

Learning to set boundaries was an essential step in my journey. I came to understand that giving must be sustainable to be truly impactful. Saying "no" or "not now" doesn't diminish generosity; instead, it allows us to give wholeheartedly when we can. This balance helped me see that caring for myself enables me to be more present, resilient, and effective in the ways I choose to give.

I've also had to recognize that, sometimes, the people we give to may not always understand or appreciate the sacrifices we make. In these moments, I remind myself that my acts of generosity are not for external validation but are guided by my own values and intentions. Realizing this shifted my perspective—it's a reminder that generosity is an offering, not an obligation, and that true giving is about sharing joy and strength, without expectation.

A Legacy of Empowerment

In my journey, I've come to see that true generosity is about creating a legacy that empowers others to stand strong and continue the cycle of giving. It's about inspiring others to believe in their own potential, to give back in their unique ways, and to make a difference in their communities.

As women, we have the unique ability to turn our struggles into strengths, our pain into purpose, and our dreams into realities. This journey of giving, for me, has been about more than just providing for others—it's about showing up authentically, standing by my values, and offering others a hand to rise alongside me. Through every story shared, every connection made, and every person uplifted, I hope to continue inspiring a generosity that is not only impactful but deeply transformative.

Embracing a Life of Generosity

As I look back on my journey, I realize that generosity is more than an action—it's a way of life, a daily commitment to lifting others and ourselves. It's about giving from a place of wholeness, fueled by empathy and resilience. The most impactful acts of generosity don't require grand gestures; often, they come from the small, consistent ways we show up for each other.

For me, generosity has become an ongoing practice of self-reflection and intention. Every day, I set aside time to ask myself: Who can I uplift today? What unique strength or insight can I share that might ease someone else's path? Sometimes, it's a conversation, a shared story, or a reminder of their potential. Other days, it's simply listening, offering a space of understanding.

I encourage you to embrace this journey of giving in your own life. Start by looking inward—ask yourself what strengths you possess, what lessons you've learned, and how you might share those with others. Generosity isn't always about tangible resources; often, it's our time, our words, and our compassion that carry the most impact.

Together, let's build a world where generosity is woven into the fabric of our daily lives, where we see our stories and strengths not just as our own but as gifts to uplift others. Remember, the act of giving is a ripple—each gesture, big or small, has the power to reach far beyond what we might imagine. So, let's take that first step every day, and in doing so, inspire others to do the same.

Hanna Olivas

Founder and CEO of SHE RISES STUDIOS

https://www.linkedin.com/company/she-rises-studios/
https://www.facebook.com/sherisesstudios
https://www.instagram.com/sherisesstudios_llc/
www.SheRisesStudios.com

Author, Speaker, and Founder. Hanna was born and raised in Las Vegas, Nevada, and has paved her way to becoming one of the most influential women of 2022. Hanna is the co-founder of She Rises Studios and the founder of the Brave & Beautiful Blood Cancer Foundation. Her journey started in 2017 when she was first diagnosed with Multiple Myeloma, an incurable blood cancer. Now more than ever, her focus is to empower other women to become leaders because The Future is Female. She is currently traveling and speaking publicly to women to educate them on entrepreneurship, leadership, and owning the female power within.

A Life of Gratitude, Love, and Impact

By Hanna Olivas

There's something undeniably powerful about the act of giving. It reaches deep into the soul, connecting us to one another in ways that transcend words, wealth, or status. When we give, we don't just offer something material or temporary; we extend a piece of our heart, a reflection of our deepest values, and in return, we receive something far greater than what we've offered. Giving is a journey, one that can transform not just the lives of those we touch but also our own.

This is my story—the journey of giving that has shaped me, molded me, and transformed the way I view the world. It's not just about giving to causes or charities, but about giving in everyday life—giving love, kindness, hope, and inspiration. Through the lens of my own experiences, I've come to believe that the greatest impact we can make in this world isn't measured by dollars or material things. It's measured by the love we give, the gratitude we show, and the way we lift others along the way.

I wasn't born with a silver spoon in my mouth—far from it. My life started with humble beginnings, raised by a single mother and grandparents who didn't graduate high school. From an early age, I witnessed what it meant to struggle, to sacrifice, and to live in a world where the odds seemed stacked against you. But I also learned something else—something far more valuable than money or material wealth. I learned the power of giving.

My grandmother, though we had little, was the kind of woman who would give you the shirt off her back if you needed it. She'd give her time, her love, her patience, and whatever small comforts she could afford. Her heart was bigger than our bank account, and through her,

I learned that true wealth isn't about what you have, but about what you give.

One memory sticks with me as if it happened yesterday. I was about ten years old, and we were living in a modest home, struggling to make ends meet. One day, a neighbor knocked on the door. She was in tears, explaining that her husband had just lost his job, and they didn't have enough money to buy groceries for their three children. Without hesitation, my grandmother went to our kitchen, gathered what little food we had, and handed it to the woman. I remember feeling conflicted—on the one hand, I was proud of my grandmother's generosity. But on the other hand, I was scared. I knew we didn't have much ourselves, and I worried about what we would eat.

When the woman left, I asked my grandmother why she gave so much when we had so little. She smiled, knelt down to my level, and said, "Hanna, when you give, you never go without. What you give will come back to you in ways you can't even imagine."

At the time, I didn't fully understand what she meant. But as the years passed, I began to see that giving wasn't just about material things. It was about love, kindness, compassion, and faith. And the more you gave, the more your heart expanded. The more you gave, the richer your life became—not in dollars, but in joy, connection, and purpose.

As I grew older, the lessons I learned from my grandmother stayed with me, shaping the woman I would become. I started several businesses, faced the trials of entrepreneurship, and worked hard to build a life that my family could be proud of. Along the way, I learned that success wasn't just about financial achievements. It was about how I could use my success to impact others.

I remember the first time I was able to give in a way that truly changed someone's life. I had just launched one of my companies, and we were finally starting to see some financial success. One day, a single mother

I knew from the community confided in me that she was struggling to pay for her children's school supplies. She was doing everything she could to make ends meet, working two jobs, but it still wasn't enough. I saw the exhaustion in her eyes, the weight of the world on her shoulders.

Without a second thought, I told her I would take care of it. I went to the store and filled up two carts with school supplies, backpacks, clothes, and even a few fun extras for her kids. When I delivered them to her home, she burst into tears. But it wasn't the school supplies that moved her—it was the feeling that someone cared. It was the realization that she wasn't alone in her struggle.

In that moment, I understood something profound: Giving isn't just about meeting a need. It's about lifting a person's spirit. It's about saying, "I see you. I care about you. You matter." And when we do that—when we give in a way that touches someone's soul—it creates a ripple effect. That mother, inspired by the kindness she received, went on to volunteer at her children's school, helping other parents who were struggling. And so, the cycle of giving continued.

Over the years, my journey of giving has evolved in ways I never could have imagined. What started as small acts of kindness grew into something much larger, something that has become a cornerstone of my life's purpose. Through my work with Brave and Beautiful Blood Cancer Foundation, I've had the incredible privilege of connecting with individuals and families who are facing one of the hardest battles anyone can go through—the battle with cancer. Blood cancers like leukemia and lymphoma are devastating, not only to the patient but to their families as well. The journey is filled with fear, uncertainty, and often, financial hardship.

But it's also a journey that can be filled with hope, strength, and an outpouring of love—if we choose to give. That's why through the

Brave and Beautiful Blood Cancer Foundation, we focus on giving in tangible, meaningful ways. We organize care packages, toy drives, turkey drives, and coat drives, all aimed at supporting not just the patients but their families as well. The impact of these simple acts of kindness is immeasurable. A care package can brighten a child's day in the hospital, a turkey can provide a sense of normalcy during a holiday season when everything else feels out of control, and a warm coat can offer comfort in the cold months when a family is struggling to make ends meet.

These are the moments where giving goes beyond just meeting a need. It becomes about restoring dignity, lifting spirits, and providing hope. One of the most profound experiences I've had through this foundation was during one of our toy drives. A mother approached me with tears in her eyes, holding the hand of her young son, who was battling leukemia. She told me how much it meant to her that we had thought of families like hers during such a difficult time. "You gave my son a reason to smile," she said. "In all the darkness, you brought light."

In that moment, I understood that giving is so much more than just an exchange of goods or money. It's about showing up for people when they need it most. It's about being a source of light in someone's darkest hours. And when you give in that way—when you give from the heart, without expecting anything in return—you not only change the lives of others, but you also transform your own life.

The Brave and Beautiful Blood Cancer Foundation has become one of the most meaningful expressions of giving in my life. It's a way for me to honor the journey of so many brave individuals battling cancer, but it's also a way to remind myself of the power of love and generosity. We often think of giving as something we do for others, but the truth is, giving transforms us. It humbles us, fills us with gratitude for the blessings we have, and reminds us of our shared humanity.

One of the most profound aspects of my giving journey has been learning to give not only in times of abundance but also in times of personal struggle. In 2018, I was diagnosed with multiple myeloma, a type of blood cancer. In a cruel twist of fate, the very disease I had been working to support others through had now become a part of my own story. Suddenly, I was on the other side, experiencing the fear, the pain, and the uncertainty that so many others had shared with me.

It would have been easy to turn inward during that time, to focus on my own battle and retreat from the world. But instead, I found that the more I gave, the stronger I became. I poured my heart into the foundation, determined to use my own journey as a way to inspire others. I organized more toy drives, more turkey drives, more care packages—anything I could do to remind others that they weren't alone, that even in the hardest of times, there is always a reason to keep going.

Through this process, I came to understand that giving isn't just about what we do for others. It's about how we heal ourselves. It's about finding strength in vulnerability, power in love, and purpose in the journey.

The impact of giving is far-reaching, and it's not always visible. Sometimes, the seeds we plant take time to grow, and we may never see the full extent of the difference we've made. But that's the beauty of giving—it's not about immediate rewards or recognition. It's about faith. It's about trusting that every act of kindness, every gift of love, will create ripples that extend far beyond what we can imagine.

One of the most powerful lessons I've learned through the Brave and Beautiful Blood Cancer Foundation is that giving isn't just about material goods. It's about giving time, attention, and love. Some of the most meaningful moments I've experienced have come from sitting with families, listening to their stories, and offering them a shoulder to lean on. In those moments, I realized that giving isn't always about what we can physically provide. It's about presence—about being there for someone in their time of need, showing up even when it's uncomfortable or difficult, and giving the gift of your attention, your empathy, your love. Sometimes, a simple act of kindness can be more powerful than anything else. Sitting beside a parent who feels lost as their child fights cancer, listening to their fears, their hopes, and their heartbreak—that's giving, too.

Through my journey, I've come to understand that we all have something to give. Whether it's our time, our resources, or our compassion, we all have the power to make a difference. And when we give without expectation, we unlock a deeper purpose in our lives. The beauty of giving is that it doesn't have to be grand or extravagant. It can be small—small, but significant.

One year, during our Thanksgiving turkey drive, we were able to provide meals for dozens of families who were struggling to put food on the table. I remember one family in particular—a single mother with three young children. When we handed her a turkey and the fixings for a holiday meal, she began to cry. She told me that she had been praying for a miracle, and that she didn't know how she was going to provide for her children that Thanksgiving. She didn't expect anyone to help, but she held onto hope.

That encounter stayed with me. It was a reminder that what seems small to one person can be monumental to someone else. That one act of giving, that one moment of showing someone they are seen, cared for, and supported, can change the trajectory of their lives. It can restore their faith in humanity, their belief that good things can happen, and their hope for a better future.

My journey of giving has taught me that we don't always need to have the answers, the perfect words, or the most extravagant resources. What we need is the willingness to be there, to show up, and to give what we can from the heart. Whether it's organizing toy drives, providing coats for the winter, or sitting beside someone in their moment of pain, we are all capable of making a difference.

And that's what makes giving so profound—it's not about perfection. It's about connection. It's about the simple act of saying, "I see you. I care about you. I'm here for you." In a world that can feel cold and disconnected, those small acts of giving become lifelines. They become the threads that weave us together in our shared humanity.

As I reflect on my journey, I realize that giving has become my way of navigating the world. It's my way of making sense of the challenges, the losses, the triumphs, and the uncertainties. Every time I give, I am reminded of my grandmother's words: "What you give will come back to you in ways you can't even imagine." She was right. Giving has filled my life with meaning, with purpose, and with a deep sense of gratitude for all that I have.

Gratitude is the cornerstone of my journey. It's the foundation upon which all giving is built. When we approach life with gratitude—gratitude for the people we love, for the opportunities we've been given, and for the ability to make a difference—we begin to see the world through a different lens. We begin to recognize the abundance in our lives, even when things are difficult. And from that place of abundance, we are able to give freely, knowing that in giving, we are only enriching our own lives.

One of the most transformative moments of my journey came when I was going through my own battle with multiple myeloma. Facing a diagnosis like that changes you. It forces you to confront your own mortality, to reassess your priorities, and to consider what truly matters in life. For me, it was a time of deep reflection, but it was also a time of immense gratitude. Gratitude for the people who stood by me, for the love that surrounded me, and for the opportunity to continue giving, even as I was going through one of the hardest battles of my life.

During that time, I leaned heavily on my faith and my belief in the power of love and generosity. I realized that even in the face of adversity, we have the power to give. We have the power to turn our pain into purpose, to use our struggles as a way to uplift others. And that's exactly what I did. Instead of retreating into my illness, I chose to lean into my purpose, to continue giving, to continue serving. Because that's what giving does—it gives us strength. It gives us hope. It gives us the ability to rise above our circumstances and become a light for others.

Through the work of the Brave and Beautiful Blood Cancer Foundation, I have seen firsthand the incredible impact that giving can have. I've witnessed the way a care package can bring joy to a child going through chemotherapy, the way a coat can provide warmth and comfort to a family during a cold winter, and the way a simple act of kindness can restore hope to someone who has lost so much.

But perhaps the greatest gift that giving has given me is the knowledge that we are never alone. In giving, we create a community—a community of love, of support, of shared humanity. We come together, not as individuals, but as a collective force for good. And in that collective, we find strength. We find hope. We find the ability to change the world, one act of kindness at a time.

As I look to the future, I am filled with hope—hope for the lives we will touch, the hearts we will uplift, and the difference we will make through the Brave and Beautiful Blood Cancer Foundation and beyond. Giving isn't just something we do once a year or during the holidays. It's a way of life. It's a journey—a journey that starts with love, gratitude, and the belief that we all have something to offer.

So, I invite you to join me on this journey of giving. To open your heart, to give freely, and to trust that what you give will come back to you in ways you can't even imagine. Together, we can create a world where love, kindness, and generosity are the norm. A world where every act of giving, no matter how small, makes a lasting impact. A world where we lift each other up, knowing that in doing so, we are lifting ourselves as well.

This is my giving journey. And it's only just begun.

In the end, giving is not about what we have, but about who we are. It's about the legacy we leave, the love we spread, and the lives we touch along the way. When we give from the heart, we change the world—not just for others, but for ourselves. So, let's keep giving, keep loving, and keep making a difference. Because, in the end, it's the giving journey that makes life truly beautiful.

Jennifer Jonassaint

Jen Inspiring Coach, LLC
President & CVO

https://lifecoachmatch.com/user/creativecoach/
https://www.facebook.com/jeninspiringcoach
https://www.instagram.com/jeninspiringcoach/
https://jeninspiringcoach.com/

With over 19 years of experience as a financial coach, I specialize in empowering women to take control of their finances and thrive in all aspects of their lives. I offer personalized strategies to help women manage family finances, navigate life transitions, and pursue their goals with confidence. My approach combines financial expertise with empathy and support to address the unique challenges women face. Together, we work towards creating a secure and fulfilling future where women can achieve their fullest potential.

Her Giving Journey Generosity

By Jennifer Jonassaint

Generosity: A Lifelong Legacy

In a world that often values individual success above all else, generosity shines as a powerful force that brings people together and changes lives. Generosity isn't just about the money you give—it's about your time, your talents, and the love you share. It's in the little moments and in the intentional choices we make every day to leave someone better than we found them.

I grew up witnessing generosity firsthand through my mother. She gave selflessly, always helping anyone in need—whether it was a meal, a ride, or a listening ear. As a child, I resented it. I often thought, "Why does she always have to give so much?" I didn't understand her deep well of kindness and felt her generosity left little room for us. But as I grew older, I started to realize the true beauty in her actions. She wasn't just giving; she was sowing seeds of love, compassion, and community.

My own journey to embrace generosity didn't happen overnight. There was a time when I believed giving was only about financial contributions, a luxury I couldn't always afford. I focused on building my career and securing my future, thinking that once I "made it," then I could give. But along the way, I discovered something incredible: you don't need wealth to give. True generosity comes from the heart, not the wallet.

A Shift in Mindset

Over 25 years ago, when I was lost in deep despair, my spiritual mom saw my heartache and stepped in. She understood my pain, yet gently urged me to look beyond myself and help someone else. At first, I was shocked and thought she didn't care. But then I learned her story—she had buried two sons, a grandson and a husband, struggled with ongoing chronic illness, and faced imminent housing challenges, yet she still consistently served those in prisons, the homeless, and single mothers in shelters. Her love and resilience left me in awe. Slowly, as I reflected on her strength, I dried my tears and began to serve despite my sadness. My situation didn't change right away; in fact, it often felt heavier. But through that act of giving, something shifted in me. I realized that even in my darkest moments, I could connect with others and find hope. My perspective transformed, and I learned that love and service could light a path through the pain, making my burden feel just a little bit lighter. This shift profoundly altered the trajectory of my life, reshaping my understanding of giving and purpose in ways I never imagined.

At this pivotal point in my life, I came to understand that generosity isn't just about random acts of kindness—it's about being intentional with how we give. I developed what I now call my "giving matrix." This framework helps me align my time, money, and talents with the causes and people I care about most. Instead of giving out of obligation or guilt, I started to give from a place of alignment with my values, purpose, and priorities.

Through this shift, I discovered the joy of giving in ways that reflect who I truly am. Whether it's donating to a charity that supports women's empowerment, offering my skills to someone in need, or simply showing up for a friend, I now give intentionally, joyfully, and with purpose.

Real-Life Generosity Examples

One story that stays with me happened when I was about ten years old. A woman in our neighborhood had recently lost her job, and it was clear that she was struggling to make ends meet. She had children to care for, and every day she walked past our house carrying heavy bags of groceries. My mother, seeing her struggling, didn't hesitate. She called out to the woman one afternoon, asking if she needed help. Not only did my mother help carry the bags, but she also invited her inside for tea. Over that simple cup of tea, a bond was formed.

So simple, yet so profound which left a lasting meaningful impression in a young mind.

It was more than just offering assistance; it was an act of seeing someone's humanity, acknowledging their struggle, and showing kindness. The woman later told us that my mother's generosity had given her the strength to keep going. She felt seen, heard, and cared for at a moment when life had made her feel invisible. That friendship grew, and years later, when our family faced hardships of our own, that same woman was the first to show up at our door with help.

At the time, I didn't grasp the significance of these moments. As a child, I sometimes felt frustrated, thinking that my mother's generosity meant less for us. I wondered why she was so quick to give when we barely had enough ourselves. But now, looking back, I see how much richer our lives were because of her kindness. Her giving didn't diminish what we had; it multiplied it. That's the magic of generosity—it creates abundance in ways we can't always measure.

It wasn't until I reached my thirties that I fully embraced the power of giving myself. Before then, I thought generosity was reserved for those with more resources than I had. I was focused on building my career, paying off debt, and achieving financial stability. I told myself that I'd give more once I reached a certain level of success. But life has a way of teaching you lessons at unexpected times.

I had a profound realization. I felt a stirring in my soul, a sense that my life was meant for something more. I began to understand that my purpose was not just about personal achievements or successes, but about serving others. This epiphany marked the beginning of my journey into volunteering.

One day, I had an opportunity to mentor a young woman who had recently moved to the United States. She was overwhelmed by the challenges of navigating life in a new country, managing her finances, and caring for her young children. I saw in her the same resilience I saw in my mother's neighbor all those years ago, but I also saw fear and uncertainty. Instead of waiting until I felt "ready" to help, I decided to dive in. I shared with her the little I knew about budgeting, managing debt, and building confidence in financial decision-making. It wasn't a grand gesture, but it was what I had to offer at that moment.

A year later, she reached out to me. She had paid off her credit card debt, started saving, and was on the path to launching a small business. Her gratitude was overwhelming, but what moved me the most was the fact that she had started mentoring others in her community. My one act of generosity had sparked a ripple effect that I hadn't anticipated. That's the beauty of giving—it doesn't stop with the person you help. It multiplies as they, in turn, help others.

I started small, helping out at local soup kitchens and food banks. But as I continued to serve, I felt a sense of fulfillment and joy that I had never experienced before. I realized that volunteering wasn't just about giving back, but about connecting with others and finding meaning in my own life.

As my faith grew, I began to put it into action and started to serve in my local church. I volunteered in the youth ministry, helping to mentor and guide young people in their spiritual journeys. I also participated in outreach programs, serving the homeless and marginalized in my community.

Through my experiences, I learned the value of generosity and the impact it can have on others. As the Bible says, "Give, and it will be given to you. A good measure, pressed down, shaken together and running over, will be poured into your lap. For with the measure you use, it will be measured to you" (Luke 6:38).

I also learned that generosity is not just about giving money or resources, but about giving our time, talents, and love. As Mother Teresa said, "It's not how much we give but how much love we put into giving."

Through my journey, I've seen the power of generosity transform lives and communities. I've seen people come together to support one another, to uplift and encourage each other. I've seen the impact that a simple act of kindness can have on someone's life.

And I've learned that generosity is not just something we do for others, but something that benefits us as well. It brings us joy, fulfillment, and a sense of purpose. It connects us to something larger than ourselves and gives us a sense of belonging.

As I continue on my journey, I'm reminded of the wisdom of Maya Angelou, who said, "Do the best you can until you know better. Then when you know better, do better." I'll keep doing better, keep giving better, and keep serving better.

The Giving Matrix: Aligning Generosity with Purpose

Creating your own giving matrix is simple. Start by reflecting on three areas of your life:

1. **Time:** How can you offer your time to make a difference? Whether it's volunteering, mentoring, or simply being there for someone, your time is one of the most valuable gifts you can give.

2. **Talents:** What skills or talents do you possess that could benefit others? Whether you're a great listener, a talented artist, or a skilled organizer, there's something only you can contribute.

3. **Money:** How can you use your financial resources to support the causes and people you believe in? No amount is too small when given with a generous heart.

By aligning your giving in these three areas with your values, you ensure that every act of kindness is meaningful and impactful. This isn't just about giving more—it's about giving in a way that reflects who you are and what you stand for.

The Ripple Effect of Generosity

Generosity has a ripple effect. One act of kindness can inspire another, creating a chain reaction that touches countless lives. I've seen this firsthand. I remember a time when I helped a struggling single mother with financial advice. I didn't expect anything in return, but years later, she told me how that moment changed her life. She went on to help others in her community, creating a ripple effect of generosity and empowerment.

My mother's legacy of giving continues to inspire me every day. Through her, I've learned that the greatest impact we can make in this world isn't through grand gestures, but through consistent, heartfelt acts of kindness. Whether it's sharing a meal with a neighbor, offering your time to a friend in need, or supporting a cause close to your heart, generosity, when practiced regularly, becomes a powerful tool for transformation.

The Generosity Challenge

I want to challenge you to embrace generosity in your own life. Start small. Today, choose one act of kindness—whether it's donating to a cause, offering your skills to someone in need, or simply reaching out to check on a friend. See how it feels to give without expecting anything in return. Notice the impact it has on others and on your own heart.

Remember the words of Mahatma Gandhi: "The best way to find yourself is to lose yourself in the service of others." Let's choose generosity, not just as a one-time act but as a way of life. The world needs your kindness now more than ever.

Dr. Sonya A. McKinzie

CEO of ThriveHER Inc.
Trauma and Recovery Coach

https://www.linkedin.com/company/thriveherinc/
https://www.facebook.com/BloggingThriveHER/
https://www.instagram.com/thriveherinc/
https://www.thriveher.me
https://linktr.ee/thriveherinc

Dr. Sonya Alise McKinzie's life is a testament to the power of perseverance and empowerment. Hailing from Brunswick, GA, she takes pride in being a devoted single mother to McKinzie Alise Baker. Despite facing the challenges of domestic violence, which led to PTSD and anxiety, these experiences have only fortified her resolve and transformed her into an emblem of fortitude. This profound personal evolution inspired her to seek higher education, culminating in degrees in Business Administration and Human Services Counseling, with an emphasis on Addictions & Recovery. Dr. McKinzie is also accredited with various certifications, including Victims Advocacy and Six Sigma (Green Belt). Come June 2024, she will be awarded a doctorate in Humanitarianism, recognizing her dedication and passion for community service.

As the visionary behind ThriveHER Inc. and ThriveHER Movement Coaching LLC, Dr. McKinzie has been celebrated with a proclamation for ThriveHER Day by the city of Brunswick, Georgia. Beyond her entrepreneurial endeavors, she is a prolific author with a passion for the arts.

The Compassionate Catalyst: Nurturing Hope and Healing through Generosity

By Dr. Sonya A. McKinzie

Lighting the Path - Generosity as Healing for Survivors of Abuse

In the safe house of compassion, every act of kindness is an inspiration of hope, a testament to the human spirit's resilience. For survivors of abuse, this kindness is not just a gentle hand; it's a powerful catalyst that can spark a journey of healing and empowerment. This chapter explores the transformative power of kindness, particularly as it relates to survivors of abuse and the role of life coaching in fostering a culture of support and empathy.

As a young girl, I was raised by my grandmother, a devout Christian and hard-working woman, in addition to my mother, who was just as Christian-facing and hardworking. I remember my grandmother cooking homemade butter pound cakes by the loaves and then giving them to her neighbors. Or you could catch her listening to and speaking life into those who were experiencing hardship. She was also quick to pray for someone at the drop of a dime. I would watch her give her last to those who came to visit her and how she never allowed anyone to leave her home without something to eat. While I did not understand then why she did that, over time, I slowly began to realize the importance of generosity and the catalyst it played in keeping peace and creating bonds.

When I ponder generosity, I think of my grandmother and my mama. You see, they taught me the importance of kindness, compassion, and being a benevolent person; they often leaned on their faith in God as a foundation. Generosity is often perceived as the giving of tangible resources, but its essence runs far deeper. It's about the intangible gifts of time, attention, and emotional support. For those who have endured abuse, these gifts can be life-changing. They provide a haven for healing and a platform for survivors to rebuild their sense of self-worth and trust in others.

At the core of generosity lies empathy, the ability to understand and share the feelings of another. Life coaches specializing in supporting abuse survivors recognize the importance of empathy. It's the bridge that connects the coach to the individual, allowing for a tailored approach that acknowledges the unique experiences and needs of each survivor.

As a woman that has both witnessed and experienced domestic abuse, it is through my faith and determination, that healing was able to begin. Through this process, I have also learned the importance of having a servant's heart and humility. You would be surprised how very important these attributes are in building your character.

Through experience, I have learned that generosity has the power to create communities that uplift and support its members. As a life coach, my role helps with the facilitation sessions where survivors can share their stories and struggles and receive care, love, and support in return. Through my nonprofit organization, I have a trauma and transformation coaching program in a place where survivors of abuse may reach out for coaching support at no charge. The programs are sponsored and therefore create an opportunity to give and pour into women and girls who have been affected by abuse.

It is in these gatherings you are not only able to share your pain but also share your successes. As survivors witness acts of kindness, they are inspired to extend the same generosity to others, creating a positive feedback loop of giving.

Life coaches play a pivotal role in guiding survivors toward a path of generosity. By modeling kindness and offering tools for self-compassion, coaches help survivors discover their capacity for generosity. This empowerment enables survivors to not only receive support but also to become sources of support for others, transforming their pain into a powerful force for communal healing.

For survivors of abuse, engaging in acts of generosity can be a significant step in their healing process. It allows them to reclaim agency and find purpose in their experiences. Generosity becomes a transformative power that not only heals the individual but also sows the seeds of empathy and kindness in the broader community.

Generosity, when ignited by a single act of kindness, can set off a chain reaction that reaches far beyond the initial gesture. For survivors of abuse, it's a beacon that lights the path to recovery and a reminder that they are not alone. Through the support of life coaches and the strength of community, survivors can harness the transformative power of generosity to create a legacy of hope and giving.

Generosity is a force that propagates far beyond the initial act. When one person steps forward to help another, it creates a ripple effect. The recipient of generosity is often moved to pay it forward, extending kindness to others in a widening circle of goodwill. This ripple effect can transform entire communities, as acts of giving become ingrained in the social fabric.

Empowering Others to Give

It is with passion that I seek to inspire others to give, it's essential to share stories of how generosity has made a difference. Public recognition of philanthropic efforts can motivate others to act. Moreover, creating opportunities for people to contribute in ways that align with their passions and skills can make giving more accessible and fulfilling.

The transformative power of generosity is twofold: it benefits the receiver and enriches the life of the giver. For the receiver, it can mean the difference between despair and hope. For the giver, it's an opportunity to grow in compassion and connect with others on a meaningful level.

Additionally, generosity helps facilitate a profound impact on our well-being, both mentally and physically. Generosity helps to foster the following actions and emotions:

1. **Reducing Stress and Anxiety:**

2. **Boosting Mood and Self-Esteem:**

    o Acts of generosity can lead to a sense of purpose and fulfillment. When we help others, it positively impacts our mood and self-esteem.

    o Feeling good about ourselves contributes to better mental health.

3. **Strengthening Social Connections:**

    o Generosity often involves interacting with others. Whether it's volunteering, donating, or simply being kind, these actions create social bonds.

    o Strong social connections are associated with better health outcomes. They provide emotional support, reduce feelings of loneliness, and enhance overall resilience.

4. **Physical Health Benefits:**

    o While the focus has been on mental health, generosity also has physical health benefits.

    o It can inspire others to be kind, creating a ripple effect. When more people engage in acts of kindness, it contributes to a healthier community.

o Although the mechanisms aren't fully understood, the positive impact on overall health is evident.

Additionally, below are some simple acts of kindness that you can practice to foster a healthier you:

1. **Smile and Greet**:

   o A warm smile and a friendly greeting can brighten someone's day. Whether it's a neighbor, a colleague, or a stranger, acknowledging their presence with kindness costs nothing but can make a significant impact.

2. **Hold the Door Open**:

   o When you're entering a building or leaving, hold the door open for the person behind you. It's a small gesture that shows consideration and thoughtfulness.

3. **Donate Unused Items**:

   o Go through your belongings and find items you no longer need. Consider donating clothes, books, toys, or household items to a local charity or shelter.

4. **Pay It Forward**:

   o Next time you're at a coffee shop or drive-thru, pay for the order of the person behind you. It creates a chain of kindness that can brighten multiple people's days.

5. **Listen Actively**:

   o Sometimes, the most generous thing you can do is lend an ear. Listen attentively when someone needs to talk. Your empathy and understanding can be incredibly valuable.

6. **Write a Thank-You Note:**

    o   Express gratitude to someone who has helped you recently. A heartfelt thank-you note can make them feel appreciated and valued.

7. **Volunteer Your Time:**

    o   Find a cause or organization you care about and volunteer your time. Whether it's serving meals at a soup kitchen, tutoring students, or helping at an animal shelter, your time and effort can make a difference.

8. **Compliment Others:**

    o   Compliments are free! If you notice something positive about someone—a new hairstyle, a job well done, or their kindness—share it with them. It boosts their confidence and spreads positivity.

9. **Offer Assistance:**

    o   If you see someone struggling with heavy bags, offer to help. Small acts of physical assistance can mean a lot to someone in need.

10. **Plant a Tree or Flowers:**

    o   Beautify your surroundings by planting a tree or flowers. It's a gift to the environment and future generations.

I would like to share a story with you where I practiced an act of kindness that triggered continuous acts of kindness even after I had long left the location.

One day, I found myself waiting in a fast-food line, frustrated because it was such a long wait. However, while sitting there, I found myself in prayer because I did not want to allow something so small and minute to allow me to ruin my entire day. When I made it to the drive-through window, I advised the employee that I wanted to pay for the person's food that was behind me. Through this act, I learned that it began a domino effect where others behind me fell in line. How do I know this? I went back the next day, and the employee remembered me and told me that this act lasted for several hours after I left the location. I began to think that simple acts of kindness made a remarkable mark on the lives of others.

Another instance was when I was sitting down on a bench, and an older lady was standing. I chose to give her my seat. It was cold and nippy out, and sitting in the spot was comfortable, but I could not ignore that a senior citizen was standing there in the cold, and I did not offer a space for her to take a seat.

After I gave her my seat, she looked at me and offered me her gloves. I told her that I could not accept them as she needed them more than I did. She said, "I insist, otherwise, I will be disappointed, and you would not want to disappoint me, would you?"

I accepted her gloves and smiled and told her, "Thank you!" Just then, she reached into her purse and pulled out another set. I was taken aback. I wondered, who carries spare mittens to give away? But I gratefully accepted them, slipping my frozen fingers into the soft fabric. They were a perfect fit.

As we chatted, I learned her name. She was on her way to work at a nearby grocery store. We shared stories about life, dreams, and the simple joys of warm pastries. When the bus arrived, she waved goodbye, leaving me with a newfound warmth—not just from the mittens but from her genuine kindness.

Over the next few weeks, I encountered her several times via text messages. Each encounter was like a mini blessing. She'd offer a cheerful greeting at the top of the morning and shared a piece of wisdom.

One day, I decided to pay it forward. I bought a box of fresh cookies from the bakery and waited at the bus stop. When my new friend arrived, I handed her the box. "For you," I said. "Thank you for being so kind."

Her eyes sparkled with surprise and gratitude. "You're a dear," she said. "Remember, kindness is like a ripple in a pond—it spreads far beyond what we can see."

From then on, our friendship blossomed. We exchanged recipes, shared laughter, and celebrated birthdays together. Mrs. Thompson taught me that generosity wasn't about grand gestures; it was about noticing the small needs around us and filling them with love.

Years later, when I moved away, she gave me a handwritten note: "Keep spreading warmth, my dear mittens friend. The world needs more kindness."

And so, I carry her legacy—the mittens, the cookies, and the wisdom—in my heart. Whenever I see someone shivering at a bus stop, I remember her and pass on the unexpected gift of warmth.

There are so many reasons why I am generous, but the primary reason is because it is what Jesus would do. I believe great things happen to us for a reason, in a season, and to teach us the importance of sharing and caring for others.

Generosity is not just an individual act; it's a collective movement that can reshape society. By choosing to give, we inspire others to do the same, creating a world where support and kindness are the cornerstones of our interactions. Let this chapter be a call to action: to embrace the transformative power of generosity and to become catalysts for change in our communities.

Krista Sobieski

Founder of Thoughtful Seed Project

https://www.linkedin.com/in/krista-sobieski-12608326/
https://www.facebook.com/kjsobieski
https://thoughtfulseedproject.com/
https://unimaginablehope.org/

Krista Sobieski is the founder of the Thoughtful Seed Project of Central Wisconsin. A farmers wife and mother of four who has a strong background in early education, leadership development and community collaborations and loves to write and share her voice. She writes about topics including life, death, parenting, fundraising, motivation, and teamwork just to hame a few. Krista lives in the country, believes in the greater God, has worked in early childhood setting for 23 years. She is the founder of Unimaginable Hope, a non-profit charity with a mission to spread kindness and bring hope to those who need it. In a moment of darkness, Unimaginable Hope was created when she lost her parents in three hours, on the same day.

Generous Hearts Help Heal the Broken: A Journey Through Grief Inspired by Kindness

By Krista Sobieski

Kindness can be transformative and from my own experience, I know that a simple act of kindness and love can change the course of the day. Kindness has a way of changing the mood for both the giver and the recipient. Practicing kindness touches our heart and makes us feel good and when we help others it can be truly soul-restoring. What I did not realize is how deeply kindness could help heal a broken heart through grief. Research has proven that doing good makes you feel good and during one of the darkest times in my life, I used kindness as my saving grace.

A study done in 2019 by Lee Rowland and Oliver Scott Curry researched and examined the effects of doing acts of kindness for both strangers and friends to determine if the positive feeling changed based on whether or not the person doing the kind deed knew the recipient. As it turns out, it makes no difference, all acts of kindness have equally positive effects on happiness, and the more of them you do, the happier you feel. There is a ripple effect to kindness and when you do something good you want to do it more often and when it's done for you, you want to pass it on. When you see and feel the effects of kindness, you want to be part of it.

My giving journey really started in 2017. It was a year that I will never forget. February 2 of that year is the day that changed my life forever. That was the day that my mother passed away from cancer and three hours later my dad unexpectedly died of a heart attack. It was the worst time in my life, as one might imagine. My mother passed away in the hospital and I found my father at their home, three hours later, to be passed out in his reclining chair, only to quickly learn that he too, passed. In my solo book, *Giving into Hope*, I share the story of my parents' deaths, but here I look forward to sharing with you how I used kindness to push through the unbearable grief, and what I learned about kindness.

The grief some days was unbearable. I tried so many things to help heal. With the support of my husband and four kids, close family, and friends I had to do something to help myself. In the months following, I recalled all the funeral cards that people shared with our family and how so many people shared the kind stories of the kind things my parents did for them. Living in grief and gratitude is not about being grateful when someone we love dies. The concept is more deeply rooted in being grateful for the time that we had with our loved ones while being thankful for the memories that remain with us after their death. It took me a while to figure that out. I was so consumed with the loss that I could not focus on the other good things around me, but I knew I needed to do something. I planted flowers in my yard, took a trip with my husband, and spent time focusing on my four children and their activities and all those things helped, but I was still feeling such a tremendous loss. I was having a hard time focusing on the good, and so consumed by the pain of losing both my parents at the same time. I understood the concept of practicing living in gratitude, yet I did not fully understand how it would allow me to heal from the pain and suffering and could not see that it really would be a transformative way of dealing with loss. When faced with tragedy, I believe it is natural to tend to focus on what we lost and the grief that follows. At times, we concentrate our energy so much on what we no longer have, that it can result in a negative focus for a long time. It is not easy to see the positive and beautiful things that are all around us. In loss-related terms, this equals yearning for what we no longer have while taking for granted the people and things still there. I was starting to have a very hard time focusing on what was right around me as I was so consumed with feeling the loss of my parents.

It's hard to be thankful after losing a loved one. After losing a loved one, being grateful is not something that many of us anticipate contemplating in the middle of our grieving. Yet, it's possible to be filled with an overwhelming outpouring of gratitude and relief following a significant loss. It's hard when you are in the heart of grief, but you can live a life filled with appreciation again after losing those you love. It took me time to understand that death can be a traumatic loss. I never thought of my parents' deaths being trauma. I didn't think about healing from it. Grief hits each person differently, and when it's a sudden loss, it's different than an entirely expected death. However, in either event, you can move forward in grief by choosing to be thankful for the time shared with your loved one versus focusing on the negative emotions tied to their loss. I lost both my parents, and how was I going to move forward from this? I had asked myself over and over again when I would start to feel normal again and how I would pass this. I realized that as I was responding to those who were there to help me, it started to make me feel better. I started to be able to feel better and show gratitude to those who were there for me. I learned that the ways we choose to show gratitude can affect the healing process and how we take action in making the decision to heal. Gratitude started to help bring together the past, present, and future to help close the gap between feeling normal and allowing myself to suffer. The feelings of gratefulness started to bring happy memories of my parents and started to make me feel better.

I knew my parents were good people but had not realized the full scope of how great they were to others beyond our family and close friends. It sparked an idea that led to the creation of a non-profit we now call Unimaginable Hope. We raise funds, write grants, and accept donations to carry on the kindness of my parents and spread it in the world as they did. We help others on many platforms to make an impact. Each spring, we host a Rockin Oldies Party, a 50s/60s dance party that raises the majority of funds we use to make a difference. My parents loved to dance, and now, through Unimaginable Hope, this event and the things we do help me carry on their legacy and spread kindness in their memory! It is rewarding and makes my heart feel better too. Their unconditional love helps me keep the promise to keep the spirit of my parents going in a way that helps others and has helped heal my broken heart. As long as you have hope, anything is possible! Even healing from traumatic grief.

It's been a learning process for me and others about how we process grief and gratitude. Both grief and gratitude aren't common emotions following a loss. They don't always follow the other. Finding peace after accepting your loss usually comes before any feelings of gratitude when trying to cope with a loss of any magnitude. It can be hard to regain your footing after a significant loss, and finding gratitude during bereavement can be a source of healing in your grief journey.

For me, the transformative power of gratitude has helped heal my grief a little each day. It somewhat forced me to live in the present and to focus only on the things that are real and present in my life at this moment.

I believe that the immeasurable power of gratitude has also helped me celebrate what I have in the here and now while acknowledging what I have lost.

The reality is that I can never physically bring my parents back. Death is real, death is forever, and it's hard to process at times, yet our loved ones can live on through how we remember them, and even more so, how we acknowledge their memory. We carry on their love through us. I struggled deeply with focusing on the hurt of the loss until I accepted that I could not change death. Right, death happens every day, and we can't change that it happens. My mother would often say, "We live to die," and that was a statement that seemed so harsh, yet the reality is, that we do live to die, and there is nothing that will stop death. Eventually, it happens to all of us. I was only robbing happiness for myself and those around me. Creating Unimaginable Hope saved me from tumbling down a deep road of despair and provided me with a positive outlook. I learned that creating a habit of living in gratitude can help you increase your feelings of happiness and overall well-being. Practicing a little bit of gratitude daily can change habits and change your perspective on your grief and suffering in the long run.

I started recognizing that there was so much to be grateful for in the little things that people do for each other every day. Appreciating even the smallest things people do for you and what you do for others helps when dealing with the challenging emotions that accompany your grief. I started to try and account for every small act of kindness or effort from others that made me feel better in my sorrow and use that to spread kindness to others. It was no longer just about me and my grief, I had others to focus on, and sharing hope and happiness with them really started to help my heart feel a little less broken and lost. Finding one bit of gratitude each day is healing. There are ways to show gratitude, even going through grief. I started to make a list of my everyday blessings and noted one small thing to be grateful for each day. It's okay to be okay, and sometimes I think that when we are going through grief, we feel guilty that we are not sad for our loved one. We sometimes suffer because it does not feel right to be happy when our loved ones die. That's backwards thinking and it's okay to be thankful for the time you had with your loved one.

I naturally find writing rewarding, and one thing that helped was writing a letter to express all that I was grateful for and why I was fortunate to have my parents' insight and unconditional love for so long. I wanted it longer, yet the gratitude is that some don't have that from their parents ever, or they lose their parents young. When we focus on the blessings, our mindset changes.

You can learn about grief and gratitude by sharing the experiences of others. The real healing started when I started sharing my story, opening up, and connecting with others. Unimaginable Hope provided me with that gift if you will—a platform to really give. Yet it was the personal connection of sharing my story and hearing others that really helped in my journey of grief.

The connection of human beings sharing is such a powerful and uplifting gift. We are inspired by others as others are inspired by us, and that is how we help each other. Though our stories are all different, it really helps you focus on where our grief stems from and also helps us understand we are not alone. Listening and talking with others about others' grief journeys and how they've worked through their loss may help you embrace your experiences.

I did find happiness after time. Some days are still hard. I deeply miss the physical presence of my parents. I miss that they are not physically here to be with us to celebrate our children and be in the stands, cheering us on. I miss their advice, their comfort, and everything about them being here with us, yet I know I can't change it. The best thing I can do in memory of them is be happy and live my life in a way that honors their memory. They would want me to thrive. When we experience gratitude, we're reminded that we can find happiness despite our pain and sorrow. Gratitude helps us embrace our grief to use it as fuel to propel us forward in our healing. Practicing gratitude is such an effective way of bringing joy back into our lives.

If you are experiencing a setback or grief like me, remember the grief will start to subside, and you may feel ready to start looking for new ways to bring joy and happiness into your life. Finding a new sense of purpose after a significant loss may help you heal from your pain, just as it did me. Unimaginable Hope helped heal my heart along with the people with whom I found a connection.

Please consider reading my book, *Giving Into Hope*, available on Amazon, or joining along on my Thoughtful Seed Project Facebook page. I am also the founder of Unimaginable Hope, a non-profit charity in memory of my parents, that has a mission to do good in this world. Other analogies I am part of include *Voices of 100 Women* and *My Unforgettable: Personal Stories That Will Inspire You*.

Karen Rudolf

Founder of Tranquil SOULutions, LLC

https://www.linkedin.com/in/tranquilsoulutions/
https://www.facebook.com/karen.rudolf.14/
https://www.instagram.com/karenrudolf_/
https://tranquilsoulutions.com/

Karen Rudolf is a transformative Life Strategist, known as a Catalyst for Change, and 6X International Best Selling Collaborative Author. Founder of Tranquil SOULutions, she is dedicated to empowering personal and professional growth through a "W"holistic approach.

With a rich background in nursing, comprehensive certifications, & licenses, Karen specializes in enhancing communication, boosting self-esteem, and fostering

"W"holistic well-being decreasing stress. Her work shifts perceptions and nurtures resilience and peace, making her a trusted guide in life's journey.

She can be reached at: www.tranquilSOULutions.com

Click the link and receive a complimentary gift from Karen

From People Pleaser to Empowered Inspirer

By Karen Rudolf

"True generosity isn't losing yourself in giving but finding strength to lift others." —K.Rudolf

In a world where giving is often equated with self-sacrifice, many women find themselves trapped in a cycle of people-pleasing. This journey is not just about generosity but redefining what it means to give to oneself. It's about understanding that genuine generosity starts from a place of self-love and empowerment.

For many years, I lived life as a people-pleaser, constantly putting others' needs before my own, believing that doing was the true essence of generosity. This current way of living took a toll on my physical well-being, leaving me feeling lonely, empty, and resentful.

My relationships, family, and role within the community began falling apart from lack of communication. What was I doing wrong? I had nothing to relateability, I had no understanding of what was happening. *That* pissed me off even more!

The effects of being a people pleaser were profound. I lost a sense of my identity, felt constant burnout, and experienced lowered self-esteem, leading to overwhelming feelings of not being enough. The turning point came when I realized that to give and inspire others truly, I had to reclaim my power and let go of the role I'd been playing.

This chapter is about that transformative journey—about learning to communicate effectively, setting boundaries, and embracing self-love.

Through my journey, I discovered that the most profound acts of generosity stem from a place of inner strength and self-mastery. By learning to master myself, I realized I could lift others in ways I'd never thought possible.

People pleasing is the tendency to prioritize others' needs and desires over your own, often at the expense of your well-being. It involves seeking validation and approval from others by constantly trying to make *them* happy. This behavior stems from a desire to feel accepted and approved and avoid conflict, and it can lead to significant personal sacrifices and a loss of one's identity.

This is my story of how I became the wind beneath others' wings, inspiring and uplifting those around me through genuine acts of generosity.

One of the most profound impacts of being a people pleaser is the gradual erosion of identity. By constantly adapting to others' expectations and desires, one loses sight of who you are.

It manifests as struggles in making decisions and empowering choices based on your preferences and values because you're so accustomed to considering what others want first.

Suppressed passions and interests: Hobbies and activities you once enjoyed may fall by the wayside as you devote more time and energy to pleasing others.

With an unclear sense of Self, over time, you may find it challenging to articulate your goals, dreams, and values as the expectations of others have been overshadowing them.

Looking back, I'd lost my voice and power of choice, resulting in my inability to make a choice and thus my inability to decide fear of being wronged or judged.

Why bother? I'm not enough anyway. I'd lost my identity of who Karen was by giving much of my power away to everyone else, leaving myself with no self-worth or esteem or feeling of having no choices on my own.

The constant effort to please everyone led me to significant physical and emotional exhaustion. This chronic state of stress can have several consequences:

Constant stress can contribute to various health problems, including headaches, gastrointestinal issues, and a weakened immune system. The relentless pursuit of approval can lead to feelings of emptiness and emotional exhaustion. Overextending yourself to meet others' needs can cause anxiety, overwhelm, and difficulty concentrating.

Back in the day, when I was nursing, caring for others became a natural part of the program. I was exhausted after working in the oncology unit and giving my all, I became burnt out and brought home not just the unfinished work but also the emotional struggles, burdens, and emotions of others. I was wearing it. I felt drained. Being an empath hadn't contributed in any way, and the people pleaser kept giving and giving and giving some more.

People pleasers often intertwine their low self-worth with the approval and validation they receive from others. This reliance on external validation can result in the inevitable failure to meet everyone's expectations, which leads to harsh self-criticism and negative self-perception. A deep-seated fear of being disliked or rejected can prevent you from asserting your needs and desires. Your sense of self-worth may become so entwined with others' opinions that you struggle to recognize and value your achievements and qualities.

After moving to Florida to raise a family, my attention turned to my former husband. I hadn't realized my love language was quality time and touch. His was being of service and affirmations. I hadn't realized how important I craved to become seen and heard our basic needs as human beings. I'd try harder and felt let down. I'd ask myself, what's wrong with me? Am I too fat? Not funny enough? I allowed myself to experience not feeling good enough, resulting in a lack of decision-making.

Crazy as it sounded, I'd be asked something as simple as where I'd like to go to dinner (yeah, quality time!!!), and then my choice would've been mixed with something like, "No, I don't want that, we'll go here." It got to the point where I'd respond, "Wherever you like, dear, whatever makes you happy." Why bother, 'I'm not enough anyway.'

I'd lost my identity of who Karen was by giving all my power away to everyone else, leaving myself with no self-worth or esteem. I was the doormat, a people pleaser. Not even able to look anyone else in the eye.

During our long divorce process, my adrenals began failing, my hair began falling out in clumps, and even during this stressful time, I continued to please the attorneys and my children, which felt as if I couldn't even succeed with them. I was so overwhelmed that I'd cry to my paralegal, who'd remind me (cha-Ching) that I was charged for his ear with my verbal vomiting. Reality check!

My best friend asked me what was next for me. What was my dream? My dream?? I couldn't even relate to a dream; I had to go to the dictionary and look up the word 'dream,' and I cried.

I had struggles with being a people pleaser after growing up with my mother being a people pleaser as well. After Mom divorced, working three jobs, she'd leave my sister and me to watch after our younger brother. I'd often cut school to have 'me' time, which resulted in me *not* hanging with the best of my peers. Pleasing my parents and teachers got me through nursing school. Caring for others became part of the program. I was exhausted after working in the oncology unit and giving my all until I burnt out.

The effects of being a people pleaser were profound. It was an ongoing perpetual cycle I had learned to feed. I believed myself to be a good wife, good mother, good pet owner, good friend, daughter, etc., and to be the best! It was my high expectations of myself that I found I could never reach the ceiling I set for myself.

It became those same expectations of what a father, husband, and marriage were supposed to look like after growing up in front of the TV version of 'Father Knows Best', my perfect role models that became too hard and difficult to match for anyone, including myself.

As a by-product, I made my husband bad and wrong and couldn't see past my construed vision. Neither of our expectations could've possibly been reached, thus failure and no understanding nor conversation, resulted in a failed marriage having an impact on all involved.

Looking back, I was in a sad state of affairs, and part of being the people pleaser was I hadn't seen a way out, and no one knew as I hadn't shared with anyone.

Many people, including people pleasers themselves, often mistake people-pleasing behavior for genuine generosity. However, there's a fundamental difference between the two:

People-pleasing is conditional: It is often driven by a desire for approval and acceptance. People pleasers give of themselves to gain something in return—whether it's praise, love, or a sense of belonging.

True generosity is unconditional: Genuine acts of generosity come from a place of abundance and self-love. They are not motivated by a need for validation but rather by a genuine desire to support and uplift others.

By understanding this distinction, you can begin to see how reclaiming your power and learning to set boundaries can lead to more authentic and fulfilling expressions of generosity.

The realization that you need to change often comes gradually, and it can also be triggered by a specific event or series of events. For many people-pleasers, the signs are always there, but they become more pronounced over time. You might start to notice:

No matter how much you rest, you never feel fully recharged. You begin to feel unappreciated or taken for granted, which leads to resentment towards those you aim to please. You start to question who you are and what you truly want in life. You realize that your own needs and desires are consistently being ignored or sacrificed. The built-up frustration can lead to unexpected emotional outbursts, often surprising yourself and those around you, not to mention a build-up of combustible tears and or expressions of frustration and anger.

For me, the realization came when the resentment grew, as I felt I was being taken for granted, and I continued to blame so many things outside myself. Allowing others to suck me dry and then resenting the fact that I allowed it, not knowing how to break the cycle, or saying the simple word, "No!" created more stress and resentment.

It kept building until one day, it became a wake-up call that made me understand the unsustainable nature of my behavior and the urgent need to reclaim my own life, which then felt selfish.

Keeping my emotions and feelings squelched, which I hadn't realized, impacted my well-being even further. As my stress began to grow and affect my health and well-being, I realized I wasn't taking care of my needs. I alone was responsible and had to be an advocate not just for myself rather also for my children.

Once the realization sets in, the catalyst for change often involves a pivotal moment or experience that pushes you to take action. These catalysts can be both external and internal:

For me, it was life coming at me fast and furious: the unknown and having to leave the familiar family home, where we were going next, disassembling a lifetime of memories and things around me became the grueling task that felt so overwhelming as well as 6-hour carpooling days. It was mentally and physically exhausting, not to mention I was doing it alone and felt it. I knew deep in my heart I wasn't meant to do life alone.

Internally, I felt as if I wanted to curl up and die. It felt like my life was over. My feelings and emotions were all over the place. I'd pray. Being a mother and in the throes of my pity party, my fears of the unknown became often paralyzing. I realized this when my paralegal, the amazing man, Cliff, reminded me very subtly that if I hadn't gotten my act together, the courts, more specifically the judge, would decide my fate and the fate of our children. I couldn't do that to them or myself! It felt as if cold water was being thrown in my face! Enough! Pitying myself wasn't supportive anymore! "Pull up Your Big Girl Panties," I'd say to myself, and something within me changed.

Driven by fear and my old patterning, and the uncertainty of a future unknown, I had to find my voice, part of what I'd lost in the process of feeling stupid, which begat my not knowing, to chronic insecurities and indecisiveness, all which irked those around me.

I was sinking fast. Something had to change, as I was feeling suffocated by the thick molasses engulfing me. I'd even felt as if I'd lost my keen sense of intuition to self-doubt. I attempted to tap in again and believed I heard communication courses. Find your voice! Be an advocate for yourself and your children.

I enrolled in personal growth and development courses as well as communication courses, vowing I'd never be out of communication again, and never looked back!

In my case, the catalyst for change was rediscovering who Karen was. This experience made it clear that I could no longer continue down the same path and that it was time to take control of my own life.

Starting the journey to reclaim your power can be daunting, but taking the first steps is crucial. These initial actions lay the foundation for lasting change and empowerment. Here are some of the first steps I took:

Self-Reflection: I began by taking time to reflect on my life and identify the patterns of people-pleasing behavior. This involved journaling my thoughts, feelings, and experiences to gain a clearer understanding of how deeply ingrained these habits were. What we resist persists, I fought journaling for years until I understood the power of self-reflection.

As I wrote my thoughts and experiences out on paper, I began asking myself questions such as, what can I learn from this experience? The lessons became invaluable, I began to slowly shift my way of being. I slowly became someone I liked.

One of the most challenging things for me to shift was the ability to realize that the word "no" was a complete sentence. "No." I'd gotten a lot of pushback from others who weren't used to me being or saying that. As I grew, I was referred to as an alien by my children, it became more challenging for them to recognize the changes and who I was becoming.

Taking back control felt strange and yet empowering. I began stretching my newfound boundaries by taking my time and found myself breathing deeper. My 'me-time' consisted of dropping my girls off at school, driving directly to the beach (the joys of FL living), not passing go, and I'd power walking the beach praying… "please God, give me strength" I'd repeat it over and over.

Be careful of what you ask for, as you'll get it. As a result of that ask, I received more challenges while others would share how strong they believed me to be, not knowing how I managed. "Managed?" I say, barely keeping one foot in front of the other.

As I reflect on the time before my divorce, there was one firm boundary I claimed for myself. Each Wednesday, I'd go to the beach, power walk, treat myself to lunch, and be back for carpool duties, which for me consisted of 3 separate school pickups totaling 6 hours of drive time each day. Do you think I deserved my time?

My former husband complained one day, "How can you go to the beach each week? You're neglecting your home chores," or "You have a horse you're neglecting." Talk about not enough. I didn't know if I was coming or going. After he said that, I made a picket sign saying "on strike," and without a word, I grabbed the car keys, turned off my phone, and disappeared for 3 hours, leaving him alone at home with the girls.

I was fuming with nowhere to go. Infuriated and a bit guilty, I came back 3 hours later, finding my voice, even in the intimidating whisper it was, and saying, "If I fall apart, this whole thing falls apart!!!" I turned on my heels and headed to the kitchen to make dinner and people please once more. Small victories, small changes, and for me, those were huge leaps.

Not knowing what I hadn't known, I realized that I couldn't do it alone, so I reached out for support from trusted friends, family members, or professionals. Joining support groups or working with a coach or therapist helped me stay accountable and provided valuable insights.

I was blaming myself for what had I done wrong to create the demise of my marriage. What was I doing wrong? Always blaming myself, my therapist, Dr Steve, who amazed me, suggested a group setting called P3 (Personal Power and Prosperity). Not only had I joined the program, but he came to the sessions to lift, guide my experience, and support the group. I was so grateful. This gave me a taste of the personal growth and development world, and since that time, I haven't looked back. I became an empowerment junkie! Determined to make a difference in my life and the lives of my girls, not ever imagining it would become a career.

My coach empowered me to make decisions and held me accountable for the things I knew I needed to get done in a timely order. My Spiritual Mentor, whom I continue to converse with to this day, steered me to go within. Each of whom I stayed with for many months if not years. The experience was invaluable.

Prioritizing self-care was essential for rebuilding my sense of self-worth. This included activities that nurtured my physical, emotional, and mental well-being, such as regular exercise, mindfulness practices, and hobbies that brought me joy. Dancing in the kitchen created a self-soothing space to calm my nervous system and something my girls and I would do together, which became a fun activity. Loved those precious moments!

My horse brought me so much joy. A confident being who was a constant listener and didn't tell me what to do or if I was wrong. I vented if he could talk… Ouch! When I'd get to see him and ride, I'd dump volumes in his ear. He'd listen patiently, often giving me a nuzzle I craved. I was so grateful for the soul connection I got to experience with Scamper. I miss that guy.

I began mindful practices such as journaling, getting in nature as much as possible, rearranging my furniture (my environment), and starting fresh. It felt good. I'd taken a closer look at my relationships and identified those that were draining versus those that were mutually supportive.

One of my then-dearest friends was going through a work challenge during the time I was going through a long, arduous divorce. Instead of choosing responsibility and dealing with the cause and effect of her actions, she went down a slippery slope of depression, drugs, and alcohol. As much as I attempted to support, soothe, and lift, my not-toughness kept getting triggered. It became draining, and with my personal life occurring, the relationship began depleting my energy. I had to release it even after 32 years of connection. It hadn't meant I hadn't loved her still; I blessed it along the way and had to move on. Creating boundaries was a form of self-love—I weeded my garden of all the nay-sayers then.

Building self-love was an ongoing process that involved affirmations, positive self-talk, and celebrating my achievements, no matter how small. I learned to appreciate and value myself for who I am, not just for what I do for myself and others.

I began putting affirmations on sticky notes on my 9' x 6' bathroom mirror long before I discovered Louise Hay's work. They covered the whole of my mirror minus a 3 x 3 square, large enough to brush my teeth and put on makeup. Each time I went to the restroom, I would read as many of these affirmations as possible.

As the days and months passed, the messages in which I'd begun to believe I'd take off the mirror and put them to the side. Just before the finalization of my divorce, I had a 3 x 3 square left on the mirror—9 sticky notes in total. The middle sticky was a reminder that I'm a child of God, and God loves me.

I began to learn that taking care of myself wasn't selfish but rather selfless. When on an airplane, one of the first things we are instructed to do is put on our masks first. It's challenging to give from a place of love when we aren't loving ourselves first.

These initial steps marked the beginning of a transformative journey that would ultimately lead to reclaiming my power and redefining generosity in my life.

I began reclaiming my power by learning slowly to express my needs and desires more clearly by taking communication courses.

Asking, knocking, building self-confidence and self-worth. My esteem for myself grew. I learned to become responsible for my words and actions. Saying things like, "I feel I heard you say x, y, z. Is that correct?" I felt I was no longer pointing the finger outside of myself. Was it easy? No, nothing ever is. We learn and grow, and now, with all my training, it still takes something. I'm still learning.

Learning to communicate effectively is a crucial step in reclaiming your power. As a people pleaser, you may have often suppressed your true thoughts and feelings to avoid conflict or to please others. However, clear and assertive communication is essential for maintaining healthy relationships and respecting your own needs.

For instance, use "I" statements to express your feelings and needs without blaming or criticizing others. For example, "I feel overwhelmed when I take on too many tasks. I need some help managing these responsibilities."

Engage in active listening by fully focusing on the speaker, acknowledging their message, and responding thoughtfully. This builds mutual respect and understanding. Be specific and direct about what you need or expect from others. Instead of saying, "I could use some help," try, "I need you to handle the grocery shopping this week because I have a lot on my plate."

Pay attention to your body language, tone of voice, and facial expressions. They can convey confidence and assertiveness without being aggressive. Role-play assertive communication in safe environments or with supportive friends to build your confidence.

Setting and maintaining boundaries is vital for protecting your well-being and ensuring that your relationships are balanced and respectful. Boundaries help you define what is acceptable and what is not, preventing others from overstepping and taking advantage of your generosity.

Saying "no" is a powerful way to assert your boundaries and prioritize your needs. It can be challenging at first, and it's essential for maintaining your mental and emotional health. Remember that saying "no" to others often means saying "yes" to yourself.

Reflect on your physical, emotional, and mental limits to understand where you need to set boundaries. Be direct and specific about your boundaries. For example, "I need uninterrupted time from 7 PM to 8 PM for my projects." is a clear communication.

Consistently enforce your boundaries to ensure they are respected. If someone crosses a boundary, calmly remind them of it. You don't always need to provide an explanation when saying "no." Simply saying, "No, I can't do that," is sufficient. Some people may resist your boundaries initially. Stand firm and reiterate your needs respectfully.

Although I'd be considered selfish by many, as they only had known me as Karen, my old way of being. I understood and although frequently still a bit defensive, my intuition had guided me to take care of me. I even learned to become less and less defensive over time learning I owe nobody an explanation unless I choose to share. Often, less is more.

Self-love is the foundation of reclaiming your power. It involves recognizing your inherent worth and treating yourself with kindness, compassion, and respect. Embracing self-love allows you to care for yourself genuinely and generously while respecting yourself in the process.

Practices Which Support You Cultivate Self-Love

Regularly affirm your worth and capabilities. Phrases like "I am deserving of love and respect" can reinforce a positive self-image.

Practice mindfulness and meditation to stay present and connected with yourself. This helps you tune into your needs and emotions. Engage in activities that nurture your body, mind, and spirit. This could include exercise, journaling, creative hobbies, or pampering yourself.

Acknowledge and celebrate your successes, no matter how small. This reinforces your sense of accomplishment and self-worth. Letting go of past mistakes and practicing self-forgiveness with self-compassion, I came to understand that growth is a continuous journey. I finally came to realize, no matter how angry or pissed off I'd gotten, my former husband had no idea why I forgave him. I did it to free myself, not him. Forgiving him and all involved released me.

By embracing self-love, I got to know not only myself, but I learned about human nature and stopped personalizing things more frequently, which empowered me and made me own my power more and more. Personal freedom became mine. I began loving life and more importantly *my* life!

True generosity begins with being kind and generous to yourself. By setting boundaries and practicing self-love, you ensure that you have the energy, resources, and emotional balance to genuinely give to others without depleting yourself.

Self-love boosts your confidence and self-worth, making you feel more capable and deserving. Healthy boundaries and effective communication lead to more balanced and respectful relationships. Prioritizing your needs reduces stress and prevents burnout, contributing to better mental health. Reclaiming your power through self-love and boundaries empowers you to make choices that align with your true self.

By practicing these things, the impact on overall well-being is enhanced greatly. Mindfulness and self-reflection are critical components of self-mastery. By being present in the moment and regularly reflecting on your thoughts and actions, you gain deeper insights into your behavior and motivations.

Incorporate mindfulness into your daily routine through meditation, deep breathing exercises, or simply taking moments to pause and focus on the present. Use journaling as a tool for self-reflection. Write about your experiences, emotions, and insights to better understand yourself and track your progress. Regularly ask yourself reflective questions like, "What are my true desires?" and "How do my actions align with my values?" to deepen your self-awareness.

After taking various personal growth and development courses, one of the common threads I'd heard over and over again was being 100% responsible for my actions. Say what?? I thought I was. It had been a challenging concept to wrap myself around until I came to learn that as long as I was pointing fingers and blaming others, I wasn't being 100% responsible.

I began self-reflection work asking myself questions such as, "What could I have done differently?" "Knowing what I know now, what will I do differently moving forward?"

It wasn't pleasant having to look in the mirror and own it, but once I did, the magic began to shift.

I stepped into forgiveness work, not just for what others had done to me, but for myself, for all I'd done with compassion to myself.

I began feeling more freedom, ease and decreased stress.

Embrace a mindset of continuous learning and growth. Recognize that self-mastery is an ongoing journey that requires dedication and a willingness to evolve. Engage in courses, workshops, and reading that expand your knowledge and skills in areas of personal interest and professional development.

Seek feedback from trusted mentors or peers to gain new perspectives and insights. Use this feedback to improve and grow. Set clear, achievable goals that align with your values and aspirations. Regularly review and adjust these goals as you progress.

I became a personal growth junkie. Instead of eating out or going away, the feeling of less stress, more awareness, and communities of like-minded individuals who have supported each other's journey became intoxicating. I craved more. For someone who couldn't look at themselves in the mirror, I began liking myself until, eventually, I realized I loved myself and who I was becoming.

Reclaiming your power leads to profound personal transformation, here are some examples of how this journey has empowered me and others.

During the divorce, 'overwhelm' was my middle name. I began learning to breathe deeply and break things down into smaller, manageable bites. Getting clear on what I was looking for in our next home, what to take, and what to release although challenging became easier, I focused on the smaller bites.

Making smaller decisions allowed me the possibility of finding a wonderful new home. I began trusting my judgments and choices. It didn't mean I hadn't fallen back occasionally; however, it was a start. The journey truly begins with the willingness to want to take that first step.

By transforming my inner world, I was open to a new relationship after believing that no one would look at me again. Who would want someone who wasn't enough? After shifting my old stories about myself, I met some wonderful people who saw my "enough-ness". As a result, I began believing it myself!

I went on to create a career around empowering others. I'd experienced the growth and power myself, and as intoxicating as it became, I believed others would enjoy the impact within their struggles and lives. As a by-product, it took focus off of myself.

Recently, one of my clients was struggling with self-worth and relationships. After a few sessions, we created an avatar he could ground himself in, and when he slipped back into the old ways of being, the simple photo on his phone reminded him who he was and he'd be back on track. It needn't be complicated, we, as humans, do enough of that already.

As you learn to master yourself and reclaim your power, the concept of generosity evolves from people-pleasing to genuine, unconditional giving and love.

Reflect on the differences between people pleasing and true generosity. People pleasing is often driven by a need for approval, while true generosity comes from a place of abundance and self-love.

After Hurricane Irma, which left many displaced communities, one of the churches in Orlando, FL, hosted many people and provided support. I believed this would be a great learning lesson for my girls, but it ended up being a life lesson for me.

In an act of true generosity, I was asked to support a financial planner in supporting the community in what's possible moving forward after devastation and recreating their lives. Yes, of course, I would, remember, I hadn't quite learned the whole idea of saying NO yet!

The planner asked us all, "Who here loves to give of themselves?" The whole room raised their hands, waving as if to say pick me, pick me! Remember, people pleasers want to be recognized and acknowledged. He leaped across the room, with a finger inches from my face, totally in my space, which had me freezing on the spot. Nowhere to go, he declared with authority, "*YOU* are *robbing* people of their joy! You are not allowing them to give to you and gain the same joy you received!"

Lesson learned!! From that moment on, I learned to simply say "thank you", releasing the thoughts of, "Oh, you shouldn't have," which, in essence, tells the other you're not worth it. That day, I also learned the importance of *giving and receiving* and allowing the generosity of others to contribute to creating a ripple effect within my world.

Self-love is the cornerstone of true generosity. When you genuinely care for and respect yourself, you can give to others from a place of abundance rather than obligation.

Self-love builds a solid foundation that allows you to live authentically. When you value yourself, you no longer feel the need to seek validation through acts of pleasing. Instead, your generosity becomes a natural extension of your inner well-being.

With a deep sense of self-worth, you experience an overflow of abundance that is now shared with others. This shift transforms giving into a joyous act rather than a burdensome duty.

Taking my newfound skill sets to a conference in South Africa, I listened as many of the teachers, in their frustration with the lack of supplies having been taken away, was a huge problem. How were they able to teach? As the creative problem solver I became, I went back the next year and was honored for making a difference in the school systems in South Africa. You never know how one thing you do will affect the masses. Never be afraid to pay it forward, it will come back tenfold!

As a result of doing the inner work and reflecting outwardly, I've since inspired and created ripples all around the world. From speaking, and presenting at conferences, to single mothers who struggle to find their passion and purpose to those who wish to advance in their careers and realize it's also been about relationships, and many others, all of whom have learned to shift their perception, look at their situations differently, and realize they had it all along, only requiring a *guide* to be the wind beneath their wings. It's all a learned skill we've yet to master as a result of not being aware. After educating myself, training, and my experiences over the years, that is who I'd become for so many.

I love seeing the butterfly effect in many as many transform their lives, seeing their eyes shine brightly, their luster and love for life return. This, in turn, brings me much joy. Giving and receiving, became joyful on so many levels for me.

Empowered by self-love, I became better equipped to recognize and nurture the potential within myself as well as those around me. This involved seeing others, becoming more of a listener, and providing the support they need to thrive.

By celebrating the achievements and successes of those around me, I support and boost others' confidence, which also fosters a supportive and uplifting environment.

My journey of self-mastery and empowerment enabled me to become a source of inspiration and support for others. Providing words of encouragement and recognition to inspire others will keep them striving towards their goals and achieving them.

I've chosen to create ripples in my life and the lives of others. As a result, I'm now on stage, being interviewed, on TV shows, podcasts, and a series of number-one best-selling collaborative books, as well as publicly recognized. Had it taken something, yes for sure as I'm an introvert, go figure!

I'm not sharing this to say, look at me, look at what I've done. I'm sharing this to say that I've been committed to making a difference in my life and the lives of others, sharing what's possible when we *choose* to transform ourselves and our lives.

As a by-product of sharing, stress mastery is learned which results in a happier, healthier body, mind, and spirit. Imagine what's possible!

The Ripple Effect of generosity and empowerment has a worldwide impact, inspiring others to also give generously and be of support to those around them by paying it forward.

As we come to the end of this chapter, it's essential to reflect on the profound journey from being a people pleaser to reclaiming your power and inspiring true generosity. This transformation is not just about shifting behaviors; it's about embracing self-love, setting healthy boundaries, and understanding that true generosity comes from a place of abundance within.

The path of reclaiming your power begins with recognizing the patterns that no longer serve you. For me, it was a journey of realizing that I could not pour from an empty cup and that my worth was not tied to how much I could give to others at the expense of myself.

Through self-reflection, setting boundaries, and cultivating self-love, I learned that the most authentic and impactful way to uplift others is by first honoring and nurturing myself.

I encourage you, dear reader, to embark on your journey of self-discovery and empowerment. It's never too late to reclaim your power, live authentically, and redefine what it means to be generous. The journey may not always be easy, but it will be deeply rewarding and transformative.

To begin this journey, start with self-reflection. Take the time to understand your needs, desires, and the patterns that hold you back. From there, work on setting and maintaining boundaries that protect your well-being and respect your time and energy. Embrace self-love by celebrating your worth and treating yourself with the kindness and compassion you deserve.

Effective communication is another critical tool in reclaiming your power. Learn to express your needs and desires clearly, concisely, and assertively, without fear of rejection or judgment. As you grow in your strength, don't forget to support and uplift those around you. True generosity is not about self-sacrifice but about sharing your abundance in a way that empowers both you and others.

By taking these steps, you will begin to reclaim your power, live authentically, and inspire generosity in others. Remember, your journey is *your* own, and it's one of the most meaningful gifts you can give generously to yourself and the world.

JOIN THE MOVEMENT!
#BAUW

Becoming An Unstoppable Woman
With She Rises Studios

She Rises Studios was founded by Hanna Olivas and Adriana Luna Carlos, the mother-daughter duo, in mid-2020 as they saw a need to help empower women worldwide. They are the podcast hosts of the *She Rises Studios Podcast* and Amazon best-selling authors and motivational speakers who travel the world. Hanna and Adriana are the movement creators of #BAUW - Becoming An Unstoppable Woman: The movement has been created to universally impact women of all ages, at whatever stage of life, to overcome insecurities, and adversities, and develop an unstoppable mindset. She Rises Studios educates, celebrates, and empowers women globally.

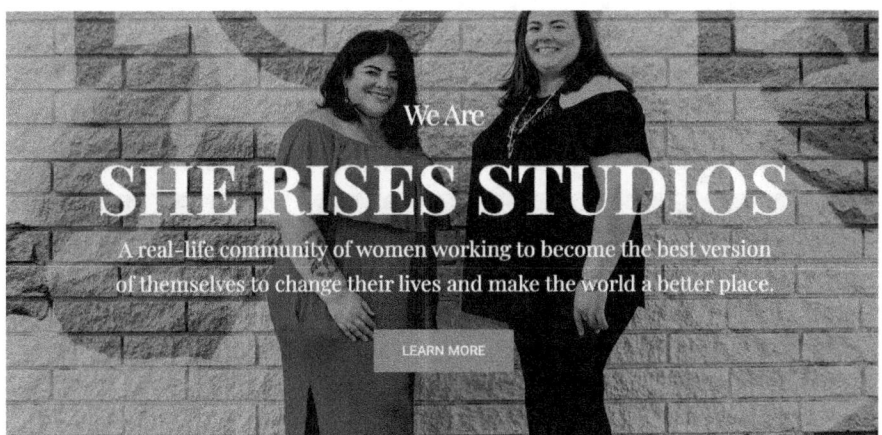

Looking to Join Us in our Next Anthology or Publish YOUR Own?

She Rises Studios Publishing offers full-service publishing, marketing, book tour, and campaign services. For more information, contact info@sherisesstudios.com

We are always looking for women who want to share their stories and expertise and feature their businesses on our podcasts, in our books, and in our magazines.

SEE WHAT WE DO

OUR PODCAST   **OUR BOOKS**   **OUR SERVICES**

Be featured in the Becoming An Unstoppable Woman magazine, published in 13 countries and sold in all major retailers. Get the visibility you need to LEVEL UP in your business!

Have your own TV show streamed across major platforms like Roku TV, Amazon Fire Stick, Apple TV and more!

Learn to leverage your expertise. Build your online presence and grow your audience with FENIX TV.
https://fenixtv.sherisesstudios.com/

Visit www.SheRisesStudios.com to see how YOU can join the #BAUW movement and help your community to achieve the UNSTOPPABLE mindset.

Have you checked out the *She Rises Studios Podcast?*

Find us on all MAJOR platforms: Spotify, IHeartRadio, Apple Podcasts, Google Podcasts, etc.

Looking to become a sponsor or build a partnership?

Email us at info@sherisesstudios.com